944
HAS

Haskins, James,
1941-

Count your way
through France.

$5.95   23938

944
HAS

Haskins, James,
1941-

Count your way
through France.

$5.95   23938

DATE	BORROWER'S NAME	

Count Your Way through
France

by Jim Haskins and Kathleen Benson

illustrations by Andrea Shine

 Carolrhoda Books, Inc. / Minneapolis

To Margaret Emily

This book is available in two editions:
Library binding by Carolrhoda Books, Inc.
Soft cover by First Avenue Editions, 1997
c/o The Lerner Publishing Group
241 First Avenue North
Minneapolis, MN 55401 U.S.A.

LIBRARY OF CONGRESS CATALOGING-IN-PUBLICATION DATA

Haskins, James.
  Count your way through France / Jim Haskins and
Kathleen Benson.
    p.   cm.
  ISBN 0-87614-874-7 (lib. bdg.)
  ISBN 0-87614-972-7 (pbk.)
  1. France—Civilization—Juvenile literature. 2. French
language—Numerals—Juvenile literature. 3. Counting—
Juvenile literature. I. Benson, Kathleen. II. Title.
DC33.7.H33 1996
944—dc20   95-36832

Manufactured in the United States of America
2 3 4 5 6 7 – SP – 02 01 00 99 98 97

Introductory Note

The French language is one of the Romance languages, which means that it came from Latin. Written French uses the Roman alphabet, just as English does, but it also uses three different accents that show how to pronounce some vowels.

French is spoken as a first language by more than 70 million people, in countries including France and all or part of Belgium, Haiti, Luxembourg, Monaco, Switzerland, Canada, and former French and Belgian colonies in Africa. After English, French is probably the most widely spoken second language in the world. French has also long been used as an international language of business as well as of education and culture.

Many French people regret the introduction of words from other languages, such as English, into the French vocabulary. In fact, a law was passed in France in 1977 that banned the use of foreign words in government documents, in ads, and on radio and TV in cases where French words could be used instead. But many English words, especially those describing popular culture (such as *jeans*) or technology (such as *computer*) are used in daily conversation.

1 un (uh)

The **one** symbol of France most familiar to people in the rest of the world is the Eiffel Tower. Designed by Alexandre-Gustave Eiffel for the Paris Exposition of 1889, it stands in a park called the Champ de Mars (shahn duh mahrs) in Paris. The tower is made up of an iron framework supported by stone pillars. It is 984 feet tall, about the height of a 70-story building. Three platforms at different heights are reached by stairs and elevators. The Eiffel Tower is a very popular tourist attraction.

2
deux (duh)

France is famous for **two** international racing competitions, one for bicycles and one for automobiles.

The Tour de France is the world's most famous bicycle race. The course winds 2,500 miles through fields and over mountains, before ending in the streets of Paris. One of the world's best-known sports car races takes place every year in the city of Le Mans. In this endurance race, drivers travel at top speed for 24 hours without stopping to refuel or change tires.

3 trois (trwa)

There are **three** stripes on the flag of France, each a different color: blue, white, and red. The flag is called the *tricolore* (tree-coh-LOHR), which means "three colors."

Before the tricolor flag was introduced, three flags were especially important to France. They were the blue flag of Saint Martin of Tours, the red flag of Saint Denis, and the white flag of Saint Joan of Arc, which later became a symbol of the kings of France. In 1789, the people of France overthrew their government. That year, the colors blue, white, and red were put together for the first time to represent France and its people. The flag underwent several changes before the present design was adopted.

4 quatre (KAT're)

Four characteristics of Gothic architecture, a building style developed in France, are flying buttresses, stained glass, pointed arches, and spires.

Flying buttresses are arched beams on the outside of a building that are used to support the walls. Colorful stained glass windows, graceful pointed arches, and spires that reach high into the sky are some of the features that make Gothic buildings so beautiful. Four of the best examples of Gothic architecture are the French cathedrals of Notre Dame (noht'r dahm), Chartres (shahrt'r), Reims (rehns), and Amiens (ah-mee-YAN).

5 cinq (sank)

There are **five** positions of the feet in ballet. Every ballet movement begins or ends with one of these positions.

Ballet, a graceful dance form, first appeared in Italy in the 1400s as part of opera. But the first ballet to combine action, music, and decoration was presented in Paris in 1581. Soon Paris was considered the capital of the ballet world.

Many of the words and phrases used in ballet are French, including *plié* (plee-AY), bending the knees outward while holding the back straight; *jeté* (zheh-TAY), a lunging jump from one foot to the other; and *en pointe* (oh pwehnt), on the toes.

six (seece)

A French child may go to as many as **six** different kinds of schools in the course of his or her education: nursery school, kindergarten, elementary school, *collège* (cah-LEHZH), *lycée* (lee-SAY), and university.

Students may leave school at the age of 16, after *collège,* which is like junior high in the United States. But if they wish to attend university, they must enroll in a *lycée,* or high school, for two or three years. The three-year program prepares students for the very difficult *baccalauréat* (bah-kah-loh-ray-AH) exam. Only if they pass the "*bac*" are students allowed to go to university.

7 sept (set)

Seven important agricultural products of France are grapes, apples, cheese, wheat, potatoes, oats, and sugar beets. France exports more farm products than almost any other country in the world. Although many of the French have left farming and moved to the city since the early 1900s, a large number of people still earn their living on small family farms.

Grapes are used to make wine, and France is a world center for wine making. Wine-grape vines were first planted in France by the Romans, who occupied the land 2,000 years ago. Two of the most famous wine-making regions, Bordeaux and Champagne, have given their names to wines.

French cheeses are also prized the world over. Hundreds of different kinds of cheeses are produced in France, including Brie, Roquefort, and Camembert.

8

huit (weet)

France shares a border with **eight** countries: Belgium, Luxembourg, Germany, Switzerland, Italy, Monaco, Spain, and Andorra. France also lies just across the English Channel from Great Britain, which makes it the geographical center of Europe. France's central position has often exposed it to war and enemy occupation. But that same location has also allowed the country to have much influence on the history and culture of its neighbors.

9 neuf (nuhf)

Nine foods for which France is known are quiche, French fries, omelettes, soufflés, mousse, pâté, croissants, crêpes, and French bread.

Quiche is a pie made with eggs and other ingredients such as cheese or ham. A soufflé is an egg dish that puffs up when it is baked. Mousse is a frothy, whipped mixture that is often a dessert. Pâté is a finely ground meat spread. Croissants are light, buttery crescent-shaped pastries. Crêpes are thin pancakes often filled with fruit.

Cooking and eating fine foods are considered noble arts in France, where great chefs become famous national figures. Many people consider French cooking to be the best in the world.

10

dix (deece)

The Arc de Triomphe (ahrk duh tree-OHMF) is a huge arch located in Paris at a place where many avenues come together. The name Arc de Triomphe means Arch of Triumph. The arch, which was built during the years from 1806 to 1836, honors the victories of French emperor Napoleon I. The people of France consider the Arc de Triomphe to be their national symbol.

The Arc de Triomphe features **ten** sculptures:

1) The Battle of Aboukir
2) General Marceau's funeral
3) The Triumph of 1810
4) The Departure of the Volunteers in 1792
5) The Capture of Alexandria
6) The Passage of the Bridge of Arcola
7) Peace
8) Resistance
9) The Battle of Austerlitz
10) The Battle of Jemmapes

Pronunciation Guide

1 / **un** / (uh)

2 / **deux** / (duh)

3 / **trois** / (trwa)

4 / **quatre** / (KAT're)

5 / **cinq** / (sank)

6 / **six** / (seece)

7 / **sept** / (set)

8 / **huit** / (weet)

9 / **neuf** / (nuhf)

10 / **dix** / (deece)

LP110   9